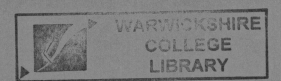

Geology Rocks!

Metamorphic Rock

Rebecca Faulkner

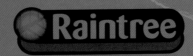

www.raintreepublishers.co.uk
Visit our website to find out more information about **Raintree** books.

To order:
☎ Phone 44 (0) 1865 888112
🖹 Send a fax to 44 (0) 1865 314091
💻 Visit the Raintree bookshop at **www.raintreepublishers.co.uk** to browse our catalogue and order online.

First published in Great Britain by Raintree,
Halley Court, Jordan Hill, Oxford OX2 8EJ,
part of Harcourt Education.
Raintree is a registered trademark
of Harcourt Education Ltd.

Editorial: Melanie Waldron and Rachel Howells
Design: Victoria Bevan
and AMR Design Ltd (www.amrdesign.com)
Illustrations: David Woodroffe
Picture Research: Melissa Allison and Mica Brancic
Production: Duncan Gilbert

Originated by Chroma Graphics Pte. Ltd
Printed and bound in China by
South China Printing Company

ISBN 978 1 406 20650 0

11 10 09 08 07
10 9 8 7 6 5 4 3 2 1

**British Library Cataloguing in
Publication Data**
Faulkner, Rebecca.
   Metamorphic Rock. – (Geology Rocks!)
   552.4
A full catalogue record for this book is available
from the British Library.

Acknowledgements
The publishers would like to thank the following for
permission to reproduce photographs:

Alamy p. **38** (Beateworks Inc.), p. **39 inset** (Hugh
Threlfall), p. **29** (Tom Till); Corbis p. **11**, p. **4** (Galen
Rowell), p. **39** (PhotoCuisine/Czap), p. **36** (Reuters/
Pascal Lauener); p. **32 left** (Ric Ergenbright), p. **34**
(Richard Hamilton Smith), p. **42** (Robert Harding/
Tony Waltham), p. **43** (Tom Bean), p. **37** (Walter
Hodges); GeoScience Features Picture Library pp. **9,
13, 13 inset, 15, 21 top, 21 bottom, 33 right**,
pp. **5, 33 left** (D. Bayliss), p. **30** (Martin Land),
pp. **5 middle inset, 7, 10, 24 top, 24 bottom,
25, 26, 27, 28, 31, 35, 41, 44** (Prof. B. Booth);
Getty Images p. **12** (The Image Bank/John Lawrence);
Harcourt Education Ltd. p. **32** right (Tudor
Photography); NHPA p. **22** (Anthony Bannister),
pp. **5 top inset, 23** (Bill Coster); Science Photo
Library p. **20** (Daniel Sambraus), p. **17** (Mauro
Fermariello, p. **18** (NASA), pp. **5 bottom inset,
40** (Photo Researchers)

Cover photograph of patterns on slate, Wales
reproduced with permission of FLPA (Maurice
Nimmo).

Every effort has been made to contact copyright
holders of any material reproduced in this book.
Any omissions will be rectified in subsequent
printings if notice is given to the publishers.

Disclaimer

CONTENTS

Any words appearing in the text in bold, **like this**, are explained in the glossary. You can also look out for them in the word bank at the bottom of each page.

SQUEEZE AND HEAT

Rocks make up the ground that all life on Earth exists on – even below the oceans! But these rocks are not as steady as you might think. Over millions of years, rocks can be created, changed, and broken up.

Metamorphic rocks form when rocks are subjected to intense heat and pressure inside Earth. Over millions of years the rocks are heated so they become softer. They are then squashed, stretched, twisted, and folded. This often happens over huge areas underneath growing mountain chains. Eventually, as the overlying rocks are eroded away, the metamorphic rocks will appear at the surface of Earth.

Changing form

The word "metamorphic" comes from the Greek words *meta* (which means "change") and *morphe* (which means "form"). You may have learned about how a caterpillar **metamorphoses** into a butterfly. While not as dramatic, similar changes can occur in rocks. Rocks will alter their form when they are subjected to increased heat or pressure.

⬇ **Mount Everest, the highest mountain on Earth, is largely made of metamorphic rock.**

metamorphose change

Although most metamorphic rocks form slowly, over millions of years, in some rare cases they can be created in an instant. When lightning strikes sand, the intense heat fuses the sand grains together to form a smooth, glass-like metamorphic rock. This rock is very fragile so it is rarely found on Earth. When **meteorites** crash into the surface of Earth the intense heat and pressure from the collision cause the surrounding rocks to change into metamorphic rocks instantly.

Because metamorphic rocks have been subjected to intense heat and pressure they are very hard, durable rocks. **Marble** is one of the best-known metamorphic rocks, and it has been used for centuries to create beautiful buildings and statues.

⇨ Deep inside Earth, rocks can be heated until they are like soft clay. The pressure of the overlying rocks will bend and fold the rocks. Eventually these rocks will make their way to Earth's surface – where you can see the folds for yourself.

Find out later...

How are craters formed?

What made these mountains?

Which metamorphic rock was used to build this?

CRUST, MANTLE, AND CORE

The high temperatures and pressures needed to change rocks into metamorphic rocks are found deep inside Earth. But what is Earth like deep down below our feet?

Earth's layers

Earth is made up of layers – a bit like an onion. The **crust** is like the skin. It is a thin layer covering the surface of Earth. There are two types of crust: oceanic and continental. Oceanic crust is found beneath the oceans and is up to 10 kilometres (6 miles) thick. Continental crust is found beneath the continents and can be up to 70 kilometres (43 miles) thick. Although it is thicker than oceanic crust, continental crust is not as heavy.

Mountain crust

The crust is at its thickest under mountain ranges such as the Himalayas in northern India. Many metamorphic rocks make up the thickened crust in mountains.

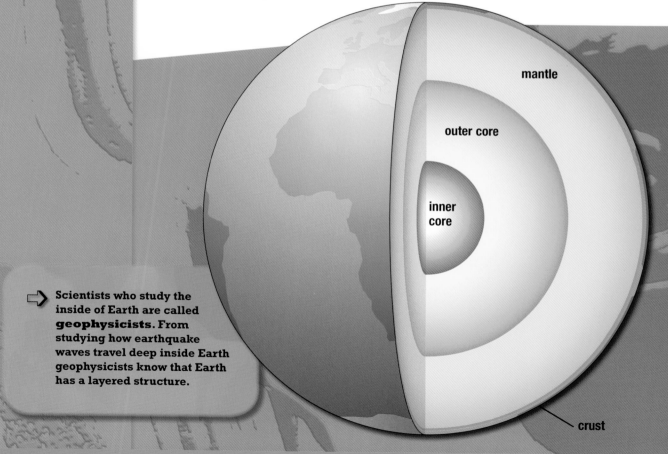

mantle

outer core

inner core

crust

➡ Scientists who study the inside of Earth are called **geophysicists**. From studying how earthquake waves travel deep inside Earth geophysicists know that Earth has a layered structure.

core central layer of Earth
crust thin surface layer of Earth

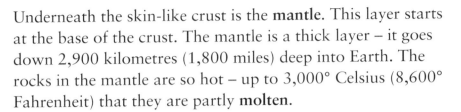

Underneath the skin-like crust is the **mantle**. This layer starts at the base of the crust. The mantle is a thick layer – it goes down 2,900 kilometres (1,800 miles) deep into Earth. The rocks in the mantle are so hot – up to 3,000° Celsius (8,600° Fahrenheit) that they are partly **molten**.

Below the mantle lies Earth's **core**. It is right at the centre of Earth and is even hotter than the mantle. No one really knows much about the core because it is too deep for us to study. We do know, however, that there is an inner and outer core. The inner core is solid, and the outer core is liquid.

Hot rocks!
The searing hot temperatures of the lower crust and upper mantle cause **metamorphism** of the rocks. This is a slow process that takes place over millions of years. If a rock travels too deep into the mantle it will melt completely.

⬇ **In this area of Switzerland, Earth's crust is clearly visible and we can see that it is made of rock.**

mantle   hot layer of Earth beneath the crust
molten   melted

Does the crust move?

Earth's **crust** may seem like a solid layer beneath our feet. In fact, the crust is broken up into huge, moving pieces called **plates**. Earth is covered in these plates, which fit together like a giant jigsaw puzzle.

All of the plates float on top of the **mantle** below. They are always moving very slowly over Earth. They move up to 10 centimetres (4 inches) per year, and carry the continents and oceans with them.

The plates do not all move in the same direction. In some places they are moving towards each other. One plate may slide under the other, crash into the mantle below, and melt. Chains of mountains and volcanoes often form along this kind of **plate boundary**, for example the Andes in South America.

The Himalayas

The Himalayan mountain chain formed when the land that is now India crashed violently into the Eurasian plate around 50 million years ago. The rocks in between were squeezed and crumpled to form new metamorphic rock inside the huge mountains.

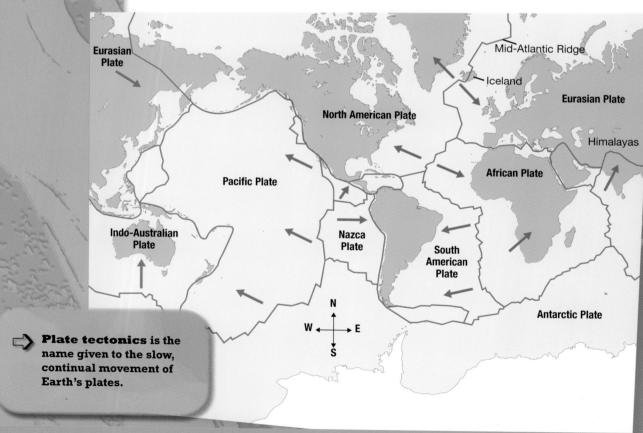

⇨ **Plate tectonics** is the name given to the slow, continual movement of Earth's plates.

igneous rock rock formed from magma either under ground or at Earth's surface

Sometimes two plates may crash into each other. When this happens the crust is squashed and folded and huge mountains, such as the Himalayas, are formed. As the rocks are squashed they experience increased pressure and heat, and so turn into metamorphic rocks.

In other places the plates are moving away from each other. This usually happens along giant mountain chains on the ocean floor, for example the Mid-Atlantic Ridge. As the plates move apart a gap (**rift**) forms between them. **Lava** rises up from the mantle to fill the gap, and cools to form new **igneous rock**.

Underwater mountains
The Mid-Atlantic Ridge is the world's longest mountain range. Most of it is under water, but it peeks out above the surface of the ocean in Iceland and the Azores. In between, it zigzags its way along the bottom of the Atlantic Ocean.

At the San Andreas Fault in California, USA, the plates are moving past each other. The Pacific plate is moving north past North America at a rate of 1–2 centimetres (0.4–0.8 inches) per year. As it does so, the pressure from the rocks sliding past each other causes them to change into metamorphic rocks.

plate giant, moving piece of crust
plate boundary edge of a plate where one plate meets another

THE WORLD'S ROCKS

Rocks are found all over the surface of Earth, from mountain ranges to the ocean floor. If you dig deep enough you will always find rock. The whole of Earth's **crust** is made of rock – even under the ice at the South Pole.

What are rocks made of?

All rocks are made of natural substances called **minerals**. There are more than 4,000 minerals on Earth, but most of these are very rare. Only about 100 minerals are commonly found in rocks.

Blue Mountains

The Blue Mountains of Jamaica have a central ridge of metamorphic rocks. They rise dramatically from the coast to a height of more than 2,250 metres (7,400 feet) at the highest point. Coffee is grown on many of the slopes of these mountains, which provide perfect growing conditions.

⬆ Rocks are found everywhere. Sometimes they create amazing landforms such as these highly **metamorphosed** rocks in the Rocky Mountains in the USA.

mineral   naturally occurring particle. Rocks are made from lots of minerals

A rock may contain many different minerals. The metamorphic rock **slate** contains the minerals quartz, feldspar, mica, and chlorite. If a rock contains hard minerals, such as quartz, it will be a hard rock. The metamorphic rock **quartzite** contains lots of quartz, so we know that it is hard.

Gneiss

The oldest rocks on Earth are a type of metamorphic rock called **gneiss**. They are found in Canada and are around 3.9 billion years old.

Rocks are made up of a mixture of different types of minerals. You can see the individual minerals in this metamorphic rock.

11

What types of rock are there?

Earth's **crust** is made up of three types of rock that are created in different ways:

- **igneous rocks**
- **sedimentary rocks**
- metamorphic rocks.

Igneous rocks are made from hot, runny material called **magma** that is found in the **mantle**. Over millions of years the magma rises up from the mantle and through Earth's crust. As it does so, it cools and hardens to form igneous rock.

Volcanic rocks

Igneous rocks are also formed when magma reaches Earth's surface. This happens when volcanoes erupt. The magma or **lava** that is thrown out of volcanoes, sometimes very violently, will eventually cool and harden to form igneous rock.

Giant's Causeway in Northern Ireland is formed from hexagonal columns of the igneous rock **basalt**. The basalt is from an ancient lava flow, and the columns form when the rock cools and fractures. There are about 37,000 columns, and they range from 40 to 50 centimetres (16 to 20 inches) across.

lava name for magma when it reaches the surface of Earth
magma molten rock from the mantle

Sedimentary rocks are formed from broken bits of other rocks. When igneous rocks are attacked by wind and rain, tiny particles are broken off and carried away by wind or in rivers. The particles are eventually deposited in a new place and build up over millions of years to form new sedimentary rock.

Metamorphic rocks are formed when heat or high pressure changes igneous or sedimentary rocks. When hot magma rises below Earth's surface it heats up the surrounding igneous rocks. This causes the rocks to change into metamorphic rocks. When mountain ranges form, the rocks are squashed and buried under the growing mountains. This means they will experience high pressure, so will change into metamorphic rocks.

Shale and sandstone

In areas where bits of mud and clay collect, they form a sedimentary rock called **shale**. In areas where sand collects a sedimentary rock called **sandstone** is formed.

⬆ This amazing rock formation is made of sandstone, a sedimentary rock. The rock has been eroded so much that only this archway is left.

⬆ Slate is a metamorphic rock that forms when shale is subjected to high pressure and is squashed into flat sheets.

The rock cycle

On Earth there is an unending cycle of rock formation, break down (**weathering**), transportation (**erosion**), and settlement in a new place (**deposition**). All these processes make up what is called the **rock cycle**.

As soon as **igneous**, **sedimentary**, and metamorphic rocks are exposed at the surface of Earth, they are attacked by weather. This is called weathering. Over millions of years, bits of rock are chipped away by wind and rain.

Recycling rocks

The surface of Earth may seem solid but, over millions of years, even the hardest rocks are worn away. In the rock cycle the materials that make up rocks are continually recycled.

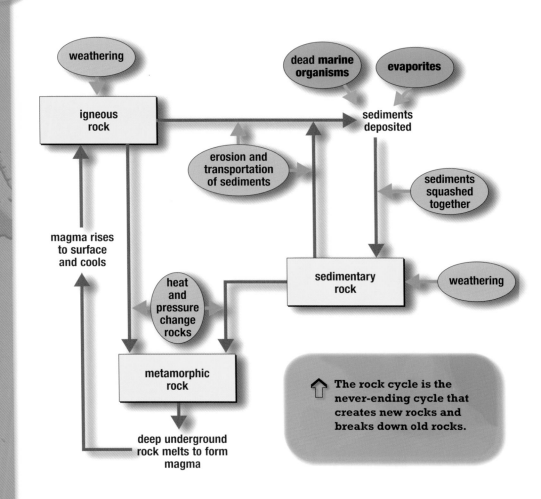

The rock cycle is the never-ending cycle that creates new rocks and breaks down old rocks.

Some of these bits of rock are small enough to be carried away to different places by the wind, rivers, or ice. This is called erosion. Eventually the bits of rock are dumped in a new place. This is called deposition. Over millions of years this deposited **sediment** changes into new rock, and the cycle starts all over again.

In areas where **plates** collide, igneous and sedimentary rocks are subjected to intense pressure and heat. Over millions of years they will change into metamorphic rock. In turn, the metamorphic rock may be heated so much that it melts to become **magma**. This magma may then rise and solidify to form igneous rock once again.

The oldest rocks

Earth is at least 4.5 billion years old, but there are no rocks left that are this old. The metamorphic rock quartzite is very hard. One of the oldest rocks that has been found on Earth is a 3.5 billion-year-old quartzite from Australia.

The lower sedimentary rock is being weathered at a faster rate than the harder, more resistant metamorphic rock on top. This creates an interesting rock formation.

MARVELLOUS METAMORPHISM

Any rock can become a metamorphic rock. Metamorphic rocks are formed when heat or high pressure changes **igneous**, **sedimentary** or metamorphic rocks that already exist. This happens deep inside Earth's **crust** in different ways.

Contact metamorphism

When hot **magma** rises below Earth's surface it heats up the surrounding rocks. These rocks are made of **minerals**. The increased heat alters some of the minerals in the rock and causes them to change into new minerals.

Magma

Magma has a temperature of about 1,000° Celsius (2,000° Fahrenheit). This is five times as hot as a very hot oven. The metamorphic rock **hornfels** forms closest to a hot blob of magma.

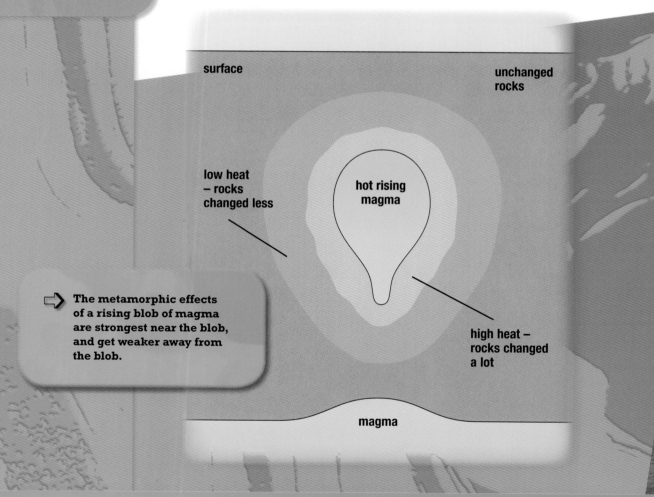

surface

unchanged rocks

low heat – rocks changed less

hot rising magma

high heat – rocks changed a lot

⇨ The metamorphic effects of a rising blob of magma are strongest near the blob, and get weaker away from the blob.

magma

impurity   substance that enters a rock during its formation and becomes part of the rock

The rocks nearest the scorching hot magma will undergo the most extreme **metamorphism,** while those further away will be less affected. Because the blob of rising magma pushes into the rocks and makes contact with them this process is called contact metamorphism. It happens deep inside Earth's crust and under volcanoes.

Marble

The metamorphic rock **marble** is formed when **limestone** is heated. Marble is usually white or yellow, but often has dark bands due to **impurities**. It is often used in buildings as it is hard and very beautiful.

↑ Marble is created when limestone is heated by contact metamorphism. The purer the limestone is the whiter the marble will be. This white marble is from a quarry in Italy. It is blasted out of the surrounding rocks using dynamite.

Regional metamorphism

When two **plates** that are slowly moving over Earth's **crust** collide, mountain ranges form along the **plate boundary**. The huge forces involved mean that the rocks are squashed, pushed upwards, or buried under the growing mountains. They will therefore experience high pressure and may also be heated, so will change into metamorphic rocks.

As this type of **metamorphism** affects rocks over a large region (area) it is called regional metamorphism. Most metamorphic rocks form in this way. You can find metamorphic rocks in the Rocky Mountains in North America, the Alps in Europe, and the Himalayas in Asia.

Forming slate

Slate is formed when **shale** experiences high pressure under a mountain range. The pressure of metamorphism squashes slate and makes it more compact and harder than shale.

When plates collide to form mountains, such as the Himalayas, intense pressure on the rocks occurs over a huge area.

The land that is now India collided with the Eurasian Plate around 50 million years ago. This caused the rocks in between to **metamorphose** and pile up to huge thicknesses, forming the highest mountains in the world – the Himalayas. India is still moving northwards today, so the huge forces involved are creating new metamorphic rock deep underground inside the mountains. One day, millions of years from now, these rocks will be exposed at the surface.

Folding rocks

Heat and high pressure can result in rocks being folded – just as you can fold a piece of paper. Folds can vary from tiny crumples to gigantic folds that may be many kilometres across.

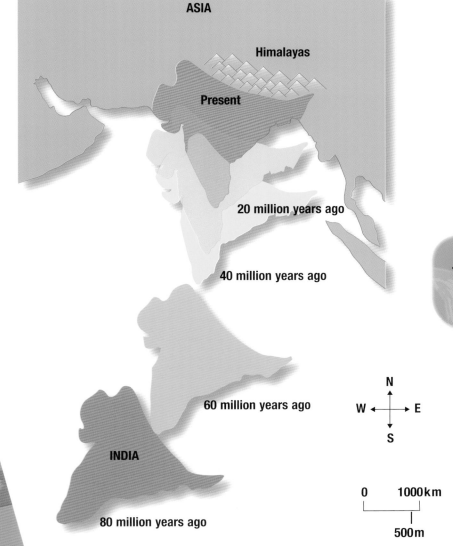

ASIA

Himalayas

Present

20 million years ago

40 million years ago

60 million years ago

N
W ←→ E
S

INDIA

80 million years ago

0   1000 km
|_____|
       |
     500 m

The Himalayas were formed when India collided with Asia.

Dynamic metamorphism

When **plates** slide past each other huge **faults** may be formed, such as the San Andreas Fault in California, USA. This has formed as the Pacific Plate grinds northwards past the North American Plate. As it does so, the pressure from the rocks sliding past each other causes them to change into metamorphic rocks. This is called dynamic **metamorphism**.

This type of metamorphism only takes place along the narrow zone around a fault. Metamorphic rocks such as **mylonite** are often formed here.

Creating friction

When two plates slide past each other they rub against each other and create friction. This causes a build up of pressure in the crust. Occasionally this pressure is suddenly released as an earthquake.

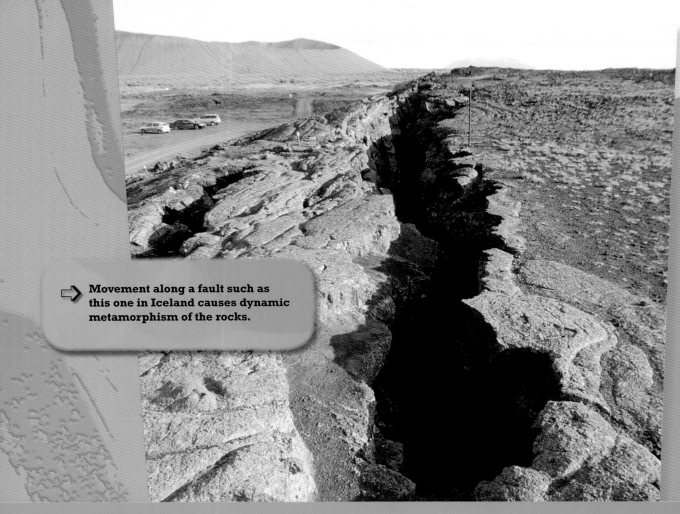

Movement along a fault such as this one in Iceland causes dynamic metamorphism of the rocks.

The Moine Thrust in the Highlands of Scotland is an example of a fault zone with highly **metamorphosed** rocks. The rocks include mylonite, **schist**, and **gneiss** as well as quartzite. The rocks have been exposed to high heat and pressure deep in the **crust** as the rocks slid past each other along the fault. As the rocks became soft they were folded into dramatic formations.

Cracking crust

A fault is formed when plate movements put the crust under so much strain that it breaks along a line of weakness. This creates a giant crack in the crust, called a fault.

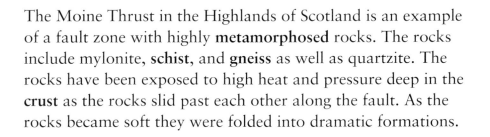

This is the Moine Thrust in Scotland. You can see the folding of the rocks.

This close-up of metamorphic rock shows how the **minerals** have been squashed due to intense heat and pressure.

Impact metamorphism

Hit by a meteorite!

In 1954 a meteorite hit a woman in Alabama, USA. Luckily the meteorite had already bounced on the ground, so she was not badly hurt.

Contact **metamorphism**, regional metamorphism, and dynamic metamorphism all take place very slowly over millions of years. One, much more rare, form of metamorphism is the kind that can happen instantly when a **meteorite** hits Earth's surface. This is called impact metamorphism.

A meteorite is a rock that has come from space and crash-landed on Earth. Before it hits Earth it is called a meteoroid. When it enters Earth's atmosphere, air resistance causes the meteoroid to heat up and form a fireball, also known as a meteor or **shooting star**.

⬇ Meteors travel towards Earth at speeds of around 80,000 kilometres (50,000 miles) per hour. Can you imagine what would happen if a meteorite like this hit Earth today?

When a meteorite hits Earth it produces a **crater**, which looks like a giant bowl. Because of the force of the impact, the meteorite itself will usually be destroyed. You may think that meteorites never actually hit Earth, but in Arizona, USA, there is some striking evidence that suggests they do. A huge impact crater, called the Barringer Meteor Crater, stretches more than 1 kilometre (0.6 miles) across the desert landscape. Many of the craters formed by meteorite impacts in the past have been eroded away over time.

As a meteor falls through Earth's atmosphere it becomes very hot. Every day, lots of small meteors make it this far, but they usually heat up so much that they **vaporize** before hitting Earth. Occasionally, however, a meteor will succeed in getting through the atmosphere. When it crashes into the surface of the **crust**, the intense heat and pressure from the collision cause the surrounding rocks to change into metamorphic rocks instantly.

Large craters
Scientists have found more than 160 large impact craters containing metamorphic rocks around the world. Two of these are Wolfe Crater in Western Australia and Chicxulub Crater in Mexico. There are also many meteorite craters hidden under the ocean.

A large meteorite crashed into Earth about 50,000 years ago and created this impact crater in Arizona, USA. The intense impact altered surrounding rocks to create new metamorphic rocks in an instant.

vaporize turn into a gas

What causes metamorphism?

Metamorphism occurs deep inside Earth's **crust**. There are two main causes of metamorphism:

- increased heat
- increased pressure.

Heat

Most metamorphic rocks you see will have been produced due to an increase in heat. The deeper you go into the crust the hotter it becomes. As a rock is heated during metamorphism the **minerals** in the rock may melt. When the rock cools again, as it moves towards the surface of the crust, new minerals will form. This happens in contact metamorphism as hot **magma** heats the rock, and also in regional metamorphism as rock is pushed deep into the crust.

Melting rocks

Most metamorphism occurs around 20 kilometres (12 miles) deep in the crust. Here the temperature is about 800° Celsius (1,800° Fahrenheit). If a rock is pushed down too deep into the crust it will completely melt. It will then become the raw material for new **igneous rock**.

Pressure and heat can turn the igneous rock **granite** (left) into the metamorphic rock **gneiss** (below). You can see how the minerals have become squashed into bands in the gneiss.

Pressure

Pressure also increases as you go deeper into the crust because there are more rocks pushing down. This means that if rocks are buried under a growing mountain range they will experience an increase in pressure. Pressure also affects rocks at **plate boundaries**. When two plates collide or slide past each other the rock is squashed and folded. All this pressure causes the minerals in the rock to become squashed and change into different minerals, therefore creating new metamorphic rock.

Mineral-rich water

Although not as important as heat and pressure, hot water containing minerals can also lead to metamorphism. Sometimes very hot water, up to 500° Celsius (1,000° Fahrenheit), can be found deep inside Earth's crust. This often happens near rising blobs of magma. This water heats the surrounding rocks and melts the minerals they contain. Some of these minerals may dissolve into the water and be removed from the rock. Other minerals contained in the water may be added to the rock to form new metamorphic rock.

Precious metals and gemstones

Precious metals, such as gold and silver, and gemstones, such as rubies and beryl, may be added to metamorphic rocks by mineral-rich water.

Hot, mineral-rich water can add some interesting minerals to rock. This metamorphic rock contains large crystals of staurolite and kyanite.

How can we classify metamorphic rocks?

The type of metamorphic rock formed in Earth's **crust** will depend on two main factors:

- the type of **parent rock**
- the **metamorphic grade**.

Parent rock

The parent rock is the type of rock that existed before **metamorphism** occurred. **Shale** is the parent rock for **slate**. Shale and slate, as well as **basalt** and **granite**, can form the parent rock for another metamorphic rock called **schist**. **Gneiss** can form from shale, slate, schist, and granite. Other common metamorphic rocks include **quartzite** and **marble**. The parent rock for quartzite is **sandstone**, and **limestone** is the parent rock for marble.

Parent rocks

Parent rock	Metamorphic rock
shale	slate
shale, slate, basalt, granite	schist
shale, slate, schist, granite	gneiss
limestone	marble
sandstone	quartzite

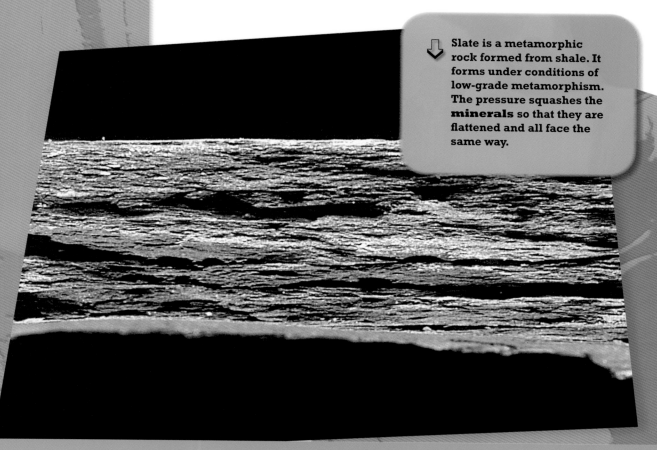

Slate is a metamorphic rock formed from shale. It forms under conditions of low-grade metamorphism. The pressure squashes the **minerals** so that they are flattened and all face the same way.

Metamorphic grade

The metamorphic grade depends on the intensity of heat and pressure a rock experiences. Rocks can show low, medium, or high-grade metamorphism. Low-grade metamorphism means the rocks only change slightly as the heat and pressure are not very intense. High-grade metamorphism means the rocks are changed dramatically due to intense pressure and heat. High-grade metamorphism will occur close to rising blobs of **magma**, while low-grade metamorphism will occur further away.

Grading rocks

All metamorphic rocks are given a grade. If the heat and pressure that formed the rock were not very intense it will only get a low grade. Low-grade metamorphism turns shale into slate. As the grade of metamorphism increases, schist forms. High-grade metamorphism produces gneiss.

The metamorphic rock gneiss forms under conditions of high-grade metamorphism. The extreme heat and pressure create new minerals in the rock.

We can classify (group) metamorphic rocks according to two other factors:

- amount of **foliation**
- grain size and **texture**.

Foliation

Metamorphic rocks can be separated into two groups depending on whether they have bands or not. Foliated rocks have their **minerals** arranged in layers. These layers are caused by increased pressure, during **metamorphism**, squashing the mineral grains into bands. Non-foliated rocks do not have these bands.

Foliated rocks

Some foliated rocks, such as gneiss, often have alternating layers of light and dark bands. These bands may also be folded — creating beautiful wavy patterns in the rock.

The layering or foliation of many metamorphic rocks is due to the intense pressure they experience while buried deep under ground.

When **granite** is subjected to increased pressure it forms the foliated metamorphic rock **gneiss**. **Marble** is an example of a non-foliated metamorphic rock.

Grain size and texture

Metamorphic rocks can also be classified by their grain size and texture. They are usually named after the texture they possess. **Fine grained** metamorphic rocks such as **slate** are said to have a slaty texture. **Coarse grained** metamorphic rocks can have either a schistose texture or a gneissose texture. Rocks displaying a schistose texture, for example **schist,** have elongated minerals. Rocks with a gneissose texture, such as gneiss, show strong banding or layering.

Different textures

If a metamorphic rock contains minerals that are all roughly the same size we say it has a granoblastic texture. If it has some large crystals set with a finer grained background we say it has a porphyroblastic texture.

This rock has a porphyroblastic texture because it has large crystals set in a fine grained background.

29

METAMORPHIC ROCK TYPES

When you look at a metamorphic rock, the first thing you will notice is whether it is banded (**foliated**) or not. For this reason, metamorphic rocks can be divided into two groups according to whether they are foliated or not.

Foliated rocks

Foliated rocks have **minerals** arranged in layers (bands). In some rocks these bands will be more obvious than others.

Gneiss

Gneiss forms from the regional **metamorphism** of mudstone, **igneous rocks,** and other metamorphic rocks. It is a coarse grained, foliated rock that often shows clear banding with alternating light and dark layers. It may also be folded. It is usually pink or grey with dark streaks and layers, and the main minerals it contains are quartz and feldspar.

Fossils

When slate is split, it will sometimes reveal highly deformed **fossils**. These fossils formed when an ancient plant or animal died and became buried in mud that hardened into shale. When the shale is **metamorphosed** into slate, many fossils may be destroyed by the intense heat or deformed by the pressure.

⬆ Slate is a low-grade metamorphic rock. It breaks up into thin sheets and may sometimes contain fossils.

fossil dead remains of a plant or animal found in a rock

Schist

There are many different types of **schist**, and they are named according to the minerals they contain. They are all foliated and often show evidence of folding. They can be fine, medium, or **coarse grained** and may have a porphyroblastic texture. The minerals are often elongated and arranged in layers as they have been squashed under high pressure.

Slate

Slate is a very **fine grained**, foliated rock formed by low-grade regional metamorpism of **shale** or mudstone. It is so fine grained that you cannot see the mineral grains without using a microscope. It is usually black or grey – sometimes with a blue or greenish tint. The main minerals it contains are quartz, mica, and chlorite. Slate has a slaty texture, which means it can be split into thin sheets along lines of weakness called cleavage planes.

Schist is a medium-grade metamorphic rock that has experienced more heat and pressure than slate.

Non-foliated rocks

The non-foliated metamorphic rocks have no layers or bands. They contain interlocking grains of **minerals** such as calcite and quartz.

Marble

Marble forms when **limestone** is subjected to intense heat and pressure during contact **metamorphism** or regional metamorphism. It is a medium grained, non-foliated rock consisting mostly of calcite. It is usually white, but may contain patches or streaks of grey, black, red, or green if it contains **accessory minerals**. If the marble has undergone low-grade metamorphism there may be highly deformed **fossils** present. At higher grades of metamorphism these will have been destroyed.

Beautiful buildings

Because marble is a beautiful rock it has been used in many grand buildings. The New York Stock Exchange in the United States has six huge marble columns on the outside of the building. The Taj Mahal in India was built between 1632 and 1654 and is made entirely from marble.

The **parent rock** for marble (left) is limestone (below). It occurs when limestone is subjected to intense heat, by a rising blob of magma, or intense pressure, from a growing mountain range.

accessory mineral   mineral that is present in a rock in very small amounts

Quartzite

Quartzite is a medium grained, non-foliated (non-banded) rock that forms when **sandstone** is **metamorphosed**. The quartz in sandstone is so tough it is not changed by metamorphism, and so quartzite consists almost entirely of the mineral quartz. It has a granoblastic texture and is white or grey in colour.

Hornfels

Hornfels is a fine grained, non-foliated metamorphic rock with a porphyroblastic texture. This means it contains both large and small crystals. It forms when mudstone or other fine grained rocks experience contact metamorphism, for example next to a rising blob of **magma**. Hornfels is usually grey or black, and sometimes has a blue or greenish tint.

Resistant rocks

Quartzite is hard and very resistant to **weathering**. Quartzite rocks therefore often form ridges and peaks in the landscape.

⬆ The parent rock for quartzite (above) is sandstone (right). As sandstone becomes deeply buried, rising temperatures will fuse the quartz grains together forming the extremely hard and weather-resistant rock quartzite.

How can we identify metamorphic rocks?

You may have seen beautiful and amazing metamorphic rocks in museums, or pictures of them in books, but how would you feel if you actually found one yourself? Would you know what it was?

Every day you will see rocks of all shapes and sizes. You can find rocks all around you – in buildings and in the natural world.

It is not always easy to tell if a rock is metamorphic or not. You will need to look at the rock closely and ask yourself a few questions.

Field guides

Learning how to identify rocks can be fun, and you can start by looking at rocks in your local area. You could use a book called a field guide to help you identify them. Field guides contain descriptions and photos of many different types of rock.

Rock outcrops are places where rock can be found naturally in the ground.

thin section very thin slice of rock mounted on a microscope slide

- Do the **minerals** all face in the same direction?
- Do the minerals look like they have been squashed?
- Are there bands or layers in the rock?
- Do the layers in the rock look twisted or folded?

If the answer to any of these questions is "yes" then the rock may well be metamorphic.

When scientists want to find out what type of rock a sample is they take very thin slices of the rock, called **thin sections**, and examine them under a microscope. When the rocks are magnified in this way, the individual minerals can be seen. Scientists can study these and use their knowledge to work out what kind of rock it is.

Finding fossils
You may occasionally find **fossils** in metamorphic rock, but they are likely to be squashed, stretched, folded, or broken up – depending on what has happened to the rock during **metamorphism**.

⬆ This is a thin section of gneiss. By looking at the rock under a microscope scientists can see which minerals it contains.

HARD BEAUTY

Now you know what metamorphic rocks look like you can see how people have used them in many different ways. You may see **slate** tiles on the roofs of houses, a **marble** work surface in your kitchen, or roads made of incredibly hard **quartzite**.

Building stones

Metamorphic rocks have endured scorching hot temperatures and enormous pressure, so some of them are very tough and are therefore very resistant to **weathering** and **erosion**. For this reason metamorphic rocks have many uses as building materials. Marble and **gneiss** are very strong and durable, so are often used as building stones.

Heavy building

One of the heaviest buildings in the world is the Palace of the Parliament in Romania. It is made from 1 million cubic metres (30 million cubic feet) of marble. The marble blocks used to build it were blasted out of the ground in Transylvania, Romania.

⇨ Gneiss is used as a building stone because it is hard and resistant to weathering, so will last a long time. The floor of this fountain is made from gneiss.

Marble is the most widely used metamorphic rock. As well as being strong and durable, it is also very beautiful and is easy to cut and polish. It has therefore been used for lots of grand buildings all over the world, including the Taj Mahal in India and the Leaning Tower of Pisa in Italy.

Marble is also used for statues and staircases – both inside buildings and outside in parks and other public places. It is also used for kitchen and bathroom surfaces and tiles because it is easy to clean, looks good, and is resistant to wear and tear.

Marble tower
The Leaning Tower of Pisa is made out of white marble. All the walls are made out of marble, and it contains 200 marble columns. The winding staircase that goes all the way to the top of the tower is also made of marble.

⬆ Marble is used in many buildings because it is a very beautiful rock. The Stock Exchange in New York, USA, is made out of white marble.

Roof tiles and rings

Slate is the perfect material to use for roof tiles, floor tiles, and paving stones, as it can easily be split into thin layers and is resistant to **weathering**. In the past it was used by schoolchildren who each had an individual writing slate and used a slate pencil to write on it. The Inuit of northern Canada also used slate to make knives.

Slate is often used to make floor tiles for kitchens and bathrooms.

Schist is used in many ways because of the **minerals** it contains. The mineral talc is found in schist. It is used to make paint, paper, and cosmetics such as make-up, soap, and baby powder. Chromium is also found in schist and is used to make stainless-steel knives and forks hard and to stop them from rusting. The "lead" in your pencil is not lead – it is a mineral called graphite. Graphite can often be found in schist.

Quartzite is very hard and is used in road and railway building. It is also used to make decorative ornaments and jewellery. The town of Quartzsite in western Arizona, USA, takes its name from the quartzite in the nearby mountains.

Jewels from rocks
Crystals of garnet and gold are often found in schist and are used to make jewellery such as rings, bracelets, and necklaces. Schist from Scotland is well known for large crystals of garnet. These are usually red, but can be yellow, green, or colourless.

Many kitchen utensils are made from stainless steel, which contains chromium extracted from the metamorphic rock schist.

This ring is made from garnet, a mineral found in many metamorphic rocks.

METAMORPHIC LANDFORMS

Although metamorphic rocks form under ground, they appear at the surface of Earth in some places where the soil and rocks above have been eroded away. They often form prominent landforms because they are tough rocks that are resistant to **weathering**.

Metamorphic mountains

The central cores of many mountain ranges across the world are made of metamorphic rocks.

Split Mountain in California, USA, shows evidence of contact **metamorphism**. The mountain has layers of **igneous** and metamorphic rock. The igneous rock formed when a blob of **magma** rose and cooled in the **crust**. At the same time, this magma heated the surrounding rocks to create metamorphic rocks. Over millions of years the overlying rocks have been eroded away, so the mountain now appears on the surface of the crust.

The Andes

The Andes mountain range is the longest mountain chain in the world. It has formed where the Nazca plate meets the South American plate along the western side of South America. The mountains contain the incredibly hard metamorphic rock **quartzite**.

This area of gneiss metamorphic rock formed deep underground. **Erosion** of the overlying rock has left it exposed on Spitsbergen Island, Norway.

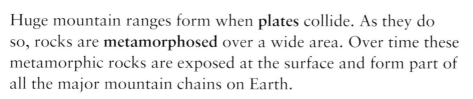

Huge mountain ranges form when **plates** collide. As they do so, rocks are **metamorphosed** over a wide area. Over time these metamorphic rocks are exposed at the surface and form part of all the major mountain chains on Earth.

The Alps were formed when the African plate collided with the Eurasian plate. The intense squeezing and heating of the rocks in-between the colliding plates resulted in the formation of **gneiss** deep in the crust beneath the developing mountains.

The Alps

You can find many outcrops of metamorphic rocks such as gneiss and **schist** in the Alps today because over millions of years they have made their way to the surface.

When plates collide the rock becomes squashed up and metamorphosed. It can form huge mountain ranges such as the Alps.

Folds and bands

Folded landforms

Folded metamorphic rock can be found all over the world – from the Rockies of North America, to the Highlands of Scotland, to the mountains of Iran.

When rocks are **metamorphosed** during mountain building or along **fault** lines they are often folded. After millions of years, these rocks will be exposed at the surface and their folds will still be there.

The mountains around the ski resort of Whistler in the Canadian Rockies are made of ancient metamorphic rocks that are 100–200 million years old. Although these rocks formed deep inside Earth at high temperature and pressure, **erosion** of the mountains over millions of years has brought these deeply buried rocks to the surface today.

⬆ Huge folds can occur when rock is subjected to high temperatures and pressure. When gneiss is folded the bands of dark and light minerals can be clearly seen.

Blackcomb Mountain is next to the town of Whistler and is a popular place to go skiing. Underneath all the snow and ice is a ridge formed of the metamorphic rock **gneiss**. This rock forms such a rugged landscape because it is hard and resistant to erosion.

The town of Whistler is built on **schist** that has clear layers or bands. These layers are formed by the **mineral** mica, which sets itself in bands during **metamorphism**.

Piles of rubble

The schist rocks around the town of Whistler are not as hard as the gneiss rocks in the surrounding mountains. They break easily along the layers, and produce piles of rubble at the bottom of cliffs.

⬇ This beautiful metamorphic rock is **quartzite**, found in an old quarry in Blue Mounds State Park, Minnesota, USA. The rock shows very clear banding.

CONCLUSION

Metamorphic rocks are not as common at Earth's surface as **igneous** and **sedimentary rocks**, but you can still find them all over the world. Some are being created under huge mountain ranges while you read this book, and at the same time older metamorphic rocks are being broken down at Earth's surface by wind, rain, and ice.

Most metamorphic rocks begin their life deep in the **crust** where heat, pressure, and hot water create them from already existing rocks. Over millions of years the overlying rock will be removed by **weathering** and **erosion** until eventually the metamorphic rock will make it to Earth's surface.

Once at the surface, metamorphic rocks often form prominent landforms such as mountains because they are tough and durable. They also reveal their amazing folds, which tell the tale of their hot and pressurized past.

There are many different types of metamorphic rock – depending on the type of rock they form from, and the **metamorphic grade**.

We have used metamorphic rocks throughout our history, and still use them today. They are used for buildings, statues, tiles, and jewellery.

A tube of **magma** has baked the rocks around it to form metamorphic rock.

FIND OUT MORE

Books

1000 Things You Should Know About Rocks and Minerals,
Chris and Helen Pellant (Miles Kelly Publishing, 2006)

Earth's Processes: Rock Cycles, Rebecca Harman
(Heinemann Library, 2006)

How We Use Materials: Rocks and Stones, Rita Storey
and Holly Wallace (Ashgate Publishing, 2006)

Rocks and Minerals, Caroline Bingham
(Dorling Kindersley, 2004)

Using the Internet

Explore the Internet to find out more about metamorphic rock.
You can use a search engine, such as www.yahooligans.com,
and type in keywords such as:
* meteorite
* lava
* marble

Websites

These websites are useful starting places for finding out more
about geology:
www.bbc.co.uk/education/rocks
www.english-nature.org.uk/geology
www.oum.ox.ac.uk/thezone
www.rocksforkids.com
www.rockwatch.org.uk

Search tips

There are billions of pages
on the Internet so it can be
difficult to find exactly what
you are looking for. These
search tips will help you
find websites more quickly:
* Know exactly what you
  want to find out about first.
* Use two to six keywords in
  a search, putting the most
  important words first.
* Be precise. Only use names
  of people, places, or things.

Glossary

accessory mineral mineral that is present in a rock in very small amounts

basalt igneous rock formed from lava flows

coarse grained large grains

core central layer of Earth

crater circular depression

crust thin surface layer of Earth

deposition laying down weathered rock in a new place

erosion removal and transport of weathered rock

evaporite sediment left behind as water evaporates

fault giant crack in Earth's crust

fine grained small grains

foliation banding

fossil dead remains of a plant or animal found in a rock

geophysicist scientist who studies the inside of Earth

gneiss metamorphic rock formed when granite is heated

granite a hard igneous rock

hornfels metamorphic rock formed during contact metamorphism

igneous rock rock formed from magma either under ground or at Earth's surface

impurity substance that enters a rock during its formation and becomes part of the rock

lava name for magma when it reaches the surface of Earth

limestone sedimentary rock made of calcite

magma molten rock from the mantle

mantle hot layer of Earth beneath the crust

marble metamorphic rock formed when limestone is heated

metamorphic grade degree of metamorphism

metamorphism process by which rocks undergo change

metamorphose change

meteorite rock that has come from space and crash landed on Earth

mineral naturally occurring particle. Rocks are made from lots of minerals

molten melted

mylonite metamorphic rock formed during dynamic metamorphism

parent rock type of rock that existed before metamorphism

plate giant, moving piece of crust

plate boundary edge of a plate where one plate meets another

plate tectonics movement of the plates across Earth

quartzite very hard metamorphic rock

rift gap between two plates

rock cycle unending cycle of rock formation and destruction

sandstone sedimentary rock made from sand

schist foliated metamorphic rock formed due to intense pressure

sediment deposited grains of rock

sedimentary rock rock formed from the broken bits of other rocks

shale sedimentary rock made from mud

shooting star name given to a meteorite when it heats up as it enters Earth's atmosphere

slate metamorphic rock formed when shale is flattened into sheets due to intense pressure

texture how something feels

thin section very thin slice of rock mounted on a microscope slide

vaporize turn into a gas

weathering breaking down of rock

INDEX